The Empowering Daily Journal Writing Package

Effective Journaling That Will Empower You for Success!

By Gina Macina

The author of *The Handbook to Happiness—A Ten-Step Challenge to Change, Achieve and Move Forward to a Happier Life!*

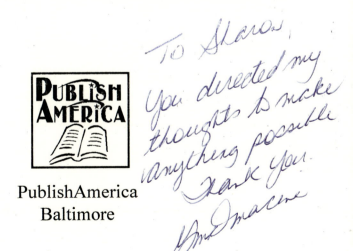

PublishAmerica
Baltimore

© 2009 by Gina Macina.
All rights reserved. No part of this book may be reproduced, stored in a retrieval system or transmitted in any form or by any means without the prior written permission of the publishers, except by a reviewer who may quote brief passages in a review to be printed in a newspaper, magazine or journal.

First printing

PublishAmerica has allowed this work to remain exactly as the author intended, verbatim, without editorial input.

ISBN: 978-1-61546-803-4
PUBLISHED BY PUBLISHAMERICA, LLLP
www.publishamerica.com
Baltimore

Printed in the United States of America

Dedication

To my children, Harrison and Leah, they are truly the most wonderful miracle that has ever been created for me.

Contents

Foreword 9

Introduction: Welcome to Your Empowering Daily Journal
    Writing Package 11

Chapter One: The Purpose of Journaling 13

Chapter Two: The Daily Shopping Lists 22

Chapter Three: Noting Positive Signs 25

Chapter Four: Make Note of Your Road Blocks 28

Chapter Five: Note Your Fearful Beliefs 35

Chapter Six: Describe Your Vision 39

Chapter Seven: The Psychology of Success and Your
    Foundation 44

Epilogue 50

Daily Journal 52

References 54

The Empowering Daily Journal Writing Package

Effective Journaling That Will Empower You for Success!

Foreword

While I was sorting through so much devastation that was occurring in my life, I became tired of just going through the motions of each new day. Everyday was the same as the last with no real change in sight. A new day would dawn and the sun would be shining, and I wasn't, I felt like I had nothing to look forward to in my future. I was left with no control over my life after so many doors had slammed on me all at once. I lost my direction and there was no one to lead me out of the maze I was in, drifting wherever the wind blew, expecting a new door to open for me without steering my own ship.

I had a sense of inferiority and I lost faith in my hopes and dreams. I had to regain my power and confidence and open new doors of opportunity for myself. I knew that I was the only one who had the answers to create a change in my life, but I didn't know where to begin.

My priority was to change my thoughts and to heal my past.

For some, when issues are left unspoken and have been laying dormant for so long the issues become blocked and are laid to rest in a place in the mind that has a sign posted "DO NOT ENTER," and are preferred to remain there. However, unconsciously these issues are the cause of present reactions to current situations and tend to pop up time and time again.

For me, I was determined to come to terms with these issues because I knew they would act as a road block along my path in life and I wanted to experience a smoother ride.

Clearing my mind of things that are stored in the "DO NOT ENTER" zone is like cleaning out my closets in my house, making room for better things to be stored. Taking down the "DO NOT ENTER" sign was crucial for my healing process to begin a happier journey.

I turned to my journal to unleash my thoughts and feelings about the past, present and the future. It was at that point when change in my life erupted like a sleeping volcano. I had clarity in my thoughts, and doors of opportunity began to open.

Introduction
Welcome to Your Empowering Daily Journal Writing Package

In *The Handbook to Happiness, a Ten-step Challenge to Change, Achieve and Move forward to a Happier Life,* I stressed the importance of maintaining a journal.

It is a private place you can rely on to empty your thoughts and feelings at the end of each day. It is your very own support system that can be called upon in an instant. It is an effective method of transforming your thoughts, renewing your mind and discovering love for yourself.

There is no fear of judgment in your journal and no need to defend yourself of the entries you write, it is for your eyes only. It is your way of removing the clutter from your mind and tracking the progress of your goals.

There are many who want to maintain a journal but do not understand its purpose and underestimate the massive effect it has on transforming irrational and unwanted thoughts into rational beliefs.

The uncertainty of where to begin is simplified in this journal package and guidance through the process is provided. I have started each day of the journal pages with hints of entries that you can complete. I have included what I have found to be successful for me, however if there are parts that you do not feel the need to fill out everyday, then don't, it is all up to you and how you want to proceed with tracking your own personal success. If there are days that you have nothing to write beside the entry, then write "nothing." There is no test at the end, as there is no end to journaling; it is simply your way of organizing your thoughts on paper.

You will notice the pages contained in this journal are not pre-printed with dates. This is done purposely so that you do not feel obligated to complete each day. Your journal is your loyal support system and will always be there for you when you feel the need.

Chapter One
The Purpose of Journaling

As a child I began writing in a diary after I was given one as a present for my birthday one year. It was one of those small little books containing blank lined paper and a flap on the outside with a small lock and key. I never really understood the purpose, the importance, or the effect it would have on my life, but I diligently wrote in it anyway. Later on I realized that my diary was my daily private session that got me through the struggle of my childhood and adolescent years. My diary helped me empty the negative thoughts that had the power to keep me awake at night and place the positive ones at the fore front of my memory.

Maintaining a daily journal is the natural profession of

everyone, as everyone has over sixty thousand separate thoughts per day rapidly running through the mind. Most of these thoughts are "automatic" thoughts that we do not consciously produce. Automatic thoughts are primarily based on our core beliefs about ourselves and require organizing, changing and releasing.

A journal is like a daily disposal service, freeing the mind of unnecessary thoughts and unveiling beliefs that are the most beneficial for a clear focus towards success. It organizes and processes information for us to use and profit from.

Writing is the salvation to clarity; it has the power to train your mind and guard it of unwanted fearful beliefs and expose your potential to change your thoughts and reveal productive ones that will allow you to concentrate on your future achievements.

Your mind is your only instrument that has the power to create what you want to appear in your life and your body takes orders from the mind. It is only with the intentions of your mind that your body will respond to and in turn will take action towards your purpose. You are responsible for what you think and your thoughts exercise your choices. Your strength to achieve your goal originates from the undivided decision of your thoughts and it is your mind's perception that your body will react upon.

A journal is a simple concept with a massive effect contributing to a happier life. If it is used effectively, it has the capacity to place your mind in the ready position for accomplishment, and readiness is the prerequisite for all goals to be achieved.

It is our illogical thoughts that keep stressful events alive and imprison our mind from obtaining peace. Your journal will show you how you can be happy by putting your mind at rest and will prepare you to create anything you want by directing your thoughts to peace, and peace of mind is where all creation begins. It will guide you and emphasize your unique qualities that will ultimately contribute to your growth towards your potential.

Escaping to a quiet place where no one will interrupt my thoughts is the only way I know how to pour everything onto a page. If throughout the course of my day I find it difficult to control my thoughts, then I will come back to my journal and continue writing. Writing is my therapeutic way of eliminating thoughts that are not constructive towards my goal. I remind myself of my goal and then quietly visualize the goal achieved and the elation I feel as a result. It is without a doubt my best solution to organize my feelings and thoughts and in the end, it will control my actions.

There are times when I hold my anger inside, allowing it to rage throughout my body like a fire out of control. My best remedy to release my hostility is by writing in my journal. I know that if I do not set it free, I will not communicate on an issue appropriately and as a result I will bring more unnecessary stress into my life.

It is important to realize how vital it is for your thoughts to be in correct order so that your actions are without regret and the art of self control will be exercised. It is easy to forget this simple remedy in the heat of the moment but if practiced often, your thoughts and feelings will be clear and the temptation to burst out in anger in a stressful situation will be limited. Learn to walk away to a quiet place to clear your mind before approaching a challenging issue. Holding your inner thoughts in without letting them go effectively can lead to stress and stress can affect the health of your body.

I had an ongoing issue I chose to turn my back on for weeks. I was confronted with this issue almost daily. For awhile I chose to ignore the source, but my anger began to fester. I was pummeled with hurt until I couldn't disregard the issue any longer and I exploded with every feeling and thought that had been running through my mind. I was being attacked personally and I allowed the situation to continue on far too long. I lost my sense of organized thoughts and self control and I was unable to stop myself to regain clarity before I spoke. I allowed my anger to take command and as a result I elevated the situation to the point of no real resolution.

It is easy to fall back onto old habits of handling issues and there will be disappointment from time to time knowing that you could have chosen your clarity of thoughts to solve the problem effectively, but decided to ignore them. Acknowledging a mistake and correcting it signifies growth. When I realized that I had handled the situation in the wrong manner, I felt compelled to write in my journal. I wanted to clear my mind of the situation and welcome the opportunity for more important thoughts to enter. I wrote the following entry:

I may have handled yesterday in the wrong manner. Both my hurt and anger became overwhelming and as a result clouded my better judgment of communication. It forced my outburst towards the issue, an approach that did not solve it. I am sorry for any distress I may have caused by my lack of control of emotions, and forgive myself for my reaction.

Your journal is a powerful tool to release negative unforgiving thoughts towards others and yourself.

I made myself aware of my reaction and the lack of clarity I displayed while trying to resolve the situation and I forgave myself through my journal by recognizing my own feelings towards the circumstance. I took responsibility for my actions by acknowledging my error in handling the issue. It doesn't matter that I didn't have the opportunity to speak these words to the people involved, all that matters is that a lesson was learned and my awareness to a better way of handling the situation was raised.

A journal gives you the opportunity to release what you should have said, instead of allowing it to block your mind and prevent more important positive thoughts to enter. It gives you the chance to liberate yourself of the situation preparing you to receive other prospective thoughts towards your goal. It will offer a sense of adequacy when you understand a lesson you are being taught in a challenging situation.

Your forgiveness and self love will become a natural habit; it will undo the past and release the future. Self love is what inspires creation and creation is a privilege of everyone.

The days that I feel overwhelmed with stress, are the most important days for me to turn to my support system, my journal. If I have a problem to solve I use what psychologists call "Narrative Therapy." I write out my problem in a story like fashion and I include a happy ending. This helps me focus positively on the end result and it alleviates the stress I feel during the process of solving the issue. An inspiring example of narrative therapy is the well known story of the great Canadian actor and comedian Jim Carey, who wrote a check to himself for ten million dollars symbolizing his success in his future acting career. He focused on a positive end result and fame and fortune followed as his career unfolded.

After my car accident I was left with many voids in my life to fill, so much had been abruptly taken away leaving me feeling empty and lost. I suffered from a loss that preoccupied my mind and held me back from my future personal development. I turned to my journal to help me change my focus and fill the gaps in my life. When you open the door for change, other opportunities seem to find their way to you.

I have a wonderful neighbor who I see each morning and evening walking her dog past our house. She is a very successful business woman, but her life never seemed to change. Each day was the same as the last. She would walk her dog, go to work, visit and care for her sick mother, come home, and walk her dog again before she turned in for the night.

One day she stopped to talk as she sometimes does and confessed she was ready for a change in her life and was placing her house on the market for sale.

Time went on and the house was still up for sale, and she was still very much open to a change in her routine life. A month later she walked by with her dog and we began to chat. She excitedly gave me the news that she was engaged to be married! I was flabbergasted as I knew she wasn't even dating anyone. She began to explain to me that out of the blue she re-connected with an old boyfriend from ten years ago, and they decided not to waste any more time apart.

My neighbor made a decision to fill a void in her life and make a change, she opened a door, and change walked in.

If you know the purpose of your goal your mind will direct your efforts to achieve it automatically. The purpose of your journal is to release unwanted thoughts and organize the ones that are beneficial to you towards accomplishing your intentions. It is a method of teaching yourself how to be happy by putting your mind at rest and giving you peace. It releases imprisoning thoughts and points you in the direction to happiness.

Chapter Two
The Daily Shopping Lists

    Not long ago I experienced many hardships in my life and I was faced with the task of putting the pieces back together again. I was devastated for so many reasons and in so many ways and I did not know where to begin to feel the peace and happiness I once enjoyed. I was overwhelmed by sadness from so many areas of my life that had been torn apart and it made me feel like I would never be whole again.

    I was advised by many people during my life crisis to take *"one day at a time."* I have always disliked that expression because I really never understood the real meaning of the phrase, then one day I found the answer and I formed my daily shopping lists.

I discovered that by setting small goals and accomplishing small tasks on a daily basis, this was what everyone meant by taking *"one day at a time."*

For each day I have included a section in the journal package called the daily **shopping list of small goals to accomplish**. I fill out this section in the morning to organize my day. At the end of the day I glance over the list and check off the items completed. The items that are not checked I carry them over to my list for the next day. As I have previously mentioned in *The Handbook to Happiness, A Ten-step Challenge to Change, Achieve and Move Forward to a Happier Life,* this is not a sprint to accomplish your goals, it is a marathon.

This daily routine enhances my focus and enables me to use my time constructively. It builds my confidence of my conviction and it trains my mind to be aligned with my goals.

You are responsible for your thoughts and your thoughts dictate your choices, choose to get into the habit of accomplishing daily as it will direct your mind of habitual success of achieving, and as a result your present situation or challenge will become less overwhelming.

Your thoughts are a system of faith and whatever you accept

in your thoughts will become reality. A daily list of small goals to accomplish will consistently confirm your faith of success.

When you have a purpose, you will achieve.

There is also a **shopping list for positive things to do for others**.

This is a list I fill out at the end of the day. It is a rewarding way to end my day knowing that I have helped create happiness for those around me.

Contributing to the goals of others intensifies and shortens the time of your own to arrive. The positive energy generated from this action will linger and will attract more of the same onto you.

When you share your thoughts and support the efforts of others to achieve, it demonstrates your abundance of love for yourself and them and love is what will create your goals and form your destiny.

"How abundantly do spiritual beings display the powers that belong to them! We look for them, but do not see them; we listen to, but do not hear them; yet they enter into all things, and there is nothing without them"
Confucius (551 BC-479 BC)

Chapter Three
Noting Positive Signs

The purpose of noting positive signs that arise towards the creation of your goal is to empower your thoughts and enforce your beliefs during the process of its development. It breaks your thoughts of worry and validates your actions to move forward with your ambitions. The appearances of positive signs are your personal feedback from reality towards your intended result. It is confirmation that your thoughts are taking action in your environment towards your goal.

At the end of each day I make a note in my journal of any positive signs indicating the progress of my goal.

Keeping track of the process encourages me to continue my journey towards its achievement. A positive sign is my evidence that the actions I have initiated towards achieving my goal are aligned with my thoughts. They are an indication that my goal is naturally falling into place and I am heading in the exact direction towards its accomplishment.

Noting positive signs is my personal method of encouragement to remain enthusiastic throughout the process of the creation of my goal. Some like to repeat positive affirmations, but repeating simple affirmations do not work for me, I find it hard to relate affirmative phrases to reality. It is my perception that my mind is trained to require proof of existence and affirmations are not real in my mind until what I visualize materializes into the physical world.

My preference is to focus on self talk of repeating my faith, hope and optimism from recent signs that have occurred. Optimism gives me the endurance that is needed to persevere towards achieving my goal. It helps me appreciate the facts that I have right now with the signs that have appeared through the opportunities I have opened up for myself.

When I look for opportunities towards the achievement of my goal, opportunities will surely emerge. Opportunities come from an open mind and habitual acceptance of saying "yes" to others. This seems like an easy method of opening yourself up to opportunity, but so many of us take ourselves out of the ready position for participation. Get yourself into the game and act on the opportunity of connecting with someone that may indirectly relay a sign to you towards your goal.

When you continually stay on task of creating your ambition, you will experience the purpose and the reason of why your goal should appear.

Chapter Four
Make Note of Your Road Blocks

Your thoughts affect reality and when your thoughts are inconsistent with your actions there is a lack of flow, or a road block towards achieving your goal. Road blocks come in the form of the way your thoughts are making you feel towards a circumstance. They will interfere with your actions and your role towards your intentions.

Nathaniel Hawthorne, a nineteenth-century writer noted, *"No man, for any considerable period, can wear one face to himself and another to the multitude without finally getting bewildered as to which may be true."*

Psychologists have a theory called cognitive dissonance reduction. It explains our motivation to justify our actions.

The principle behind this is that our attitude and thoughts become our actions and the role we play.

A famous experiment conducted in 1971 by psychologist Philip Zimbardo from Stanford University proved this theory to be correct. He wanted to see the psychological effects of becoming a prisoner or a prison guard,

He created a functional simulated prison setting in the basement of the psychology department at Standford University, where twenty four volunteers were asked to act out the roles of guards and prisoners.

Their roles were randomly chosen by the flip of a coin deciding the function of each volunteer.

The volunteers that took on the role as prisoners were formally read their rights, handcuffed and charged with their crime. They were finger printed, stripped down naked, showered and deloused for germs or lice. They were given humiliating outfits with ID numbers on the front and back to make them feel anonymous. On each prisoners right ankle was a chain bolted on and worn at all times to remind them of their role as a prisoner even when they were sleeping. They were given a stocking to put on their heads in place of shaving off their hair as done in a real prison setting.

The guards were outfitted with uniforms complete with mirrored sunglasses, clubs and whistles. They were given instructions to enforce rules of their choice that would be adhered to in a regular prison. Zimbardo himself became a part of the experiment taking on the role as prison superintendent over seeing the conduct of both the prisoners and the guards.

During the first couple of days of the experiment the behaviors of both the guards and the prisoners did not seem genuine as they acted out their roles. As time elapsed their roles then became quite authentic. Most of the guards developed indignant attitudes and developed degrading routines of punishment. The prisoners began to taunt and curse the guards and rebel. A riot broke out as the prisoners barricaded themselves in their cells pushing their beds up against the cell doors. The guards reacted by getting a fire extinguisher which shot out cold carbon dioxide and forced the prisoners away from the doors.

Less than thirty six hours into the experiment one of the prisoners began crying uncontrollably, he was filled with rage and suffered from acute emotional disturbance and disorganized thinking.

Zimbardo became just as involved in his role as prison Superintendent, as the volunteers did in their roles. A colleague of Zimbardo's dropped by to check in on the progress of the research and felt the need to remind Zimbardo that it was an experiment, and not a real prison.

The planned two week experiment was called off after only six days. It ended for two reasons, first the guards began to escalate their abuse and second Christina Maslach, a recent Stanford Ph.D. was brought into the simulated prison to conduct interviews with the volunteer guards and prisoners and she became horrified at the treatment of the prisoners and feared for the safety of the volunteers. She demanded that the experiment come to an end.

The thoughts and actions of the volunteers became so real that the volunteers lost their real identity and became their intended role in the simulated prison setting.

Zimbardo proved through his experiment that whatever thoughts we focus upon, we act upon and as a result we become and our thinking is equal to our environment.

I took the information from the results of Zimbardo's experiment and realized that whenever I feel the lack of flow towards achieving my goal, it is my thoughts that are inconsistent with my actions and the role I should be playing to accomplish my intentions.

Each time a researcher tries a technique that he has failed at, he makes a note of it so that he will not try the same practice again. Think of yourself as a researcher attempting different methods to find a cure for the thoughts that are missing to coincide with your actions towards your goal. When you notice a lack of flow in your thoughts towards your goal, then you have hit a road block, recognize it as a road block, make note of it in your journal and change your thought pattern.

"A man who has committed a mistake and doesn't correct it, is committing another mistake." Confucius **(551 BC-479 BC)**

A lack of flow can sometimes come in the form of having to force something to work as opposed to it naturally flowing together with your intentions. It is a disordered thought accompanied by guilt. When your mind is not in perfect alignment with your actions, it is saying that it is not ready for it now and it takes you out of the ready position of achieving.

An example of one of my road blocks I recently experienced was about buying a new car.

The lease on my car was about to come to an end and my partner Stuart wanted to shop around at some dealerships to see if we could get a good deal. It was not my intention to buy a new car at the time, I wasn't ready and I was feeling a little uneasy about the present economy and the volatility of our personal financial situation, but I acted upon Stuart's thoughts and went anyway.

Stuart did most of the talking to the sales people while I sat in various vehicles. We came across a car that was nice but I was still not excited as my thoughts were quite scattered, making it difficult for me to get into the role of a buyer. The salesman crunched some numbers for us and Stuart was really excited about the whole deal, but I convinced him to walk away to allow us to think about it for awhile.

Two days later we received disturbing news about Stuart's income; it was going to be cut more than one thousand dollars per month. We hit a road block. My thoughts did not match my actions and I recognized the lack of flow while we were in the environment of the dealership.

When I allow others to set my goals that are not consistent with my values, I will usually hit a road block. I paid attention to the way I was feeling at the dealership and acted accordingly.

When your thoughts match your actions everything will naturally flow without force, and is recognized in your mind as a piece of the puzzle towards your goal.

Chapter Five
Note Your Fearful Beliefs

I make a note in my journal of any fearful thoughts about the success of my goal and relinquish them with the replacement of alternative positive thoughts of my belief, truth and knowledge of achieving my goal.

Certainty is strength and fear will surrender to strength, it is only your lack of knowledge when difficulties begin to appear.

Your thoughts choose fear because you have not made the decision in your mind about your intentions and it is your perceptions that determine your actions.

It is easy to perceive anticipated events that may interfere with your plans, but usually what you fear the most will not even take place at all.

In order to correct your mind of fearful thoughts it is essential to make your decision of your goal and focus your thoughts on your belief and certainty. Gather as much knowledge as possible on your intention so that you gain confidence of your achievement.

Scattered thoughts about your goal releases fear of success and lack of focus originates from past errors that you have not forgiven yourself for. Forgive yourself for your errors and remind yourself that all errors are a learning experience. We are all here on this earth to learn and mistakes are how we are taught. As soon as you heal and forgive yourself, your thoughts of fear will be abolished. Forgiving yourself will lead to self love and self love will eliminate your fear.

It is your own perception of yourself that chooses self love and it is your ego that will interfere with self love and perceive yourself as what you wish to be rather than as you truly are, it is the perception of yourself that creates the fear to accomplish.

When you feel unworthy you are not recognizing the power of the mind and what it can do for you. Show love for yourself by accepting who you are and what you are capable of doing.

Without self love you will reject everyone and everything that is around you. Love for you will attract love from others and opportunities will follow.

Your mind is capable of creating illness through your increase of fear. Remember, only your thoughts of what you believe can create and your body reacts to the direction of your thoughts.

Replace your doubt and fearful thoughts with the knowledge you have collected through your past successful experiences and through the success of others. Try not to confuse this with comparing yourself with others, it is important to remember that when comparing yourself to others you will always come up short and thoughts of fear of your own accomplishment will enter.

Our egos will always ensure that we never measure up to the next person and therefore will set us up for failure before we even try. Our ego is a part of the belief system in ourselves. We protect our ego because the ego does not want to fail and will place fear in our mind to prevent success of the goal that is intended.

Many of our thoughts are directed by the ego and controlled

by our environment. External locus of control is when we allow our environment to control our life and let chances or outside forces determine our fate and in the end our happiness. Break away from the ego and your surroundings and adopt internal control and use your journal to change your habit of thinking.

It is habitual thoughts of failing that will cause fear and only the mind is capable of errors.

"Our greatest glory is not in never falling, but in rising every time we fall." Confucius **(551 BC-479 BC)**

Chapter Six
Describe Your Vision

What is in your heart to create and how much do you cherish it?

What idea would you like to design and mentally rehearse?

It is crucial for the answers to these questions to unfold when you are faced with making a goal decision. These are questions that must be answered before you are able to visualize and really feel the end result.

The art of visualization allows you to train your mind to develop the skill of paying attention and focusing on your potential.

I have mentioned the positive effects of narrative therapy and how it can help relieve the stress during the process of achieving your goal or resolving an issue. Narrative therapy will contribute to your thoughts and bring vision into your mind of a desirable result. An example of how this process can work occurred not too long ago when Stuart and I were faced with quite a financial dilemma.

The lawsuit from my car accident had been dragging on for almost four years with no end in sight. A mediation date would be set and then at the last minute would be cancelled for one reason or another. During the mediation process, it is the mediator's job to bring both sides to a mutually agreed amount of settlement. I had been counting on this money for a very long time, and because the case had gone on for so long we had incurred quite a debt load and there was the possibility that our house would be lost in the process.

At last another mediation date was set and this time was not cancelled. I had been holding the creditors at bay because of the anticipated settlement that would be coming and I promised to pay them after the date of mediation.

The day came and my anticipation of paying off all of my debts became real, the feeling of the relief of stress was long awaited for and the time had finally arrived.

Unfortunately things do not always work out at the exact moment of your intention and the day became a disappointment as the mediation had failed. The mediator was unable to get the two sides to agree and it was decided that the case would go to trial and let a judge decide.

I was devastated to say the least. I had all of these creditors who called me on a daily basis and my only resources to pay them were from the settlement of my case. The feeling of stress rushed through my body and became so overwhelming that I was unable to sort through my thoughts for a solution. The first thing I did when I arrived home that day was write in my journal. I needed to sort out my thoughts and have a vision in my mind of a happy ending to my financial disaster. I wrote the following:

I treasure my present environment and living conditions. I love our home and our neighbors. But my thoughts want to throw in the towel to our debts and sell our home. It would be a relief for me not to stress over paying the bills each month. I treasure the house and I treasure the relief of stress at the same time, but it seems impossible for me to have both right now.

What is my solution?

My thoughts are obviously not directing me to our much needed financial relief. I now surrender my dilemma to a higher power. It is my intention to gain clarity to make a decision for the correct action to take place.

My conviction is to feel happy and liberated of my financial burden. My vision is the feeling of relief I am going to experience when we make a decision and take action on a financial resolution in order to remain in our home and maintain our happiness.

I continued to write that day until my mind was set on a vision and free of worry. Writing helps you sort through overwhelming thoughts and will direct you to your conviction and a vision will be created. Your actions will follow and the means will be brought to you.

Your actions are a result of the intentions of your mind. Your goals are born from your thoughts and arise from conviction. Your vision is your conviction that will direct your body to respond.

The next morning after I wrote in my journal I woke up with determination on the appropriate decision of solving my problem and everything seemed to flow naturally into place. The natural flow of my phone calls that day enforced my confidence that the choice I made was the right one to follow. I made arrangements to see a financial advisor to bring resolution to our financial predicament. The financial advisor created a plan to repay our debt comfortably and at the same time we would still be able to remain living in our home.

At the end of each day I write a detailed description of the goal I intend to achieve and the vision I have of the goal. I illustrate the end result of my goal and what it will look like in my life after it has been achieved. It is important for me to know exactly what I want to appear and the purpose it will serve me when it arrives. My visualization can also help me through any thoughts of fear that may creep into my mind. If I have a clear vision of my goal then my fearful thought will disappear.

Chapter Seven
The Psychology of Success and Your Foundation

Your personal foundation is developed through the fulfillment of basic human needs. These fulfilled needs form our thoughts and direct our behavior. They enable growth and develop characteristics in our personality and motivate us to move forward to our highest potential of success.

During my early studies in psychology I was fascinated and found myself relating to a theory that was proposed in 1943 called *A Theory in Human Motivation*, by Dr. Abraham Maslow, a humanist psychologist.

Dr. Maslow believed that humans were capable of reaching their highest potential and had the ability to choose the direction of their lives if they progressed through a series of developmental stages that meet various basic human needs. He understood that if these needs went unsatisfied the mind would be preoccupied until the need was fulfilled. As an example, your physiological need of food and water, if you are really thirsty then your thirst will preoccupy your mind until it is quenched.

Maslow's theory of hierarchy of needs was based on a compiled list of forty eight influential people, who shared the same personality characteristics and who he considered to be fully self-actualized. Among these people he studied included Abraham Lincoln, Albert Einstein, Franklin D. Roosevelt, Ludwig von Beethoven, Eugene V. Debs, Amelia Earhart and Jane Addams.

He concluded in his study that self-actualizers share sixteen personality characteristics that enable them to grow and develop to their potential. They contribute to their growth and learn from negative experiences.

Maslow's discovery of the common characteristics of a self-actualizer is as follows:

1. Do not distort reality
2. Have a high level of self-acceptance
3. Have loving and intimate relationships with others
4. Are autonomous and independent
5. Are spontaneous in thought and emotion
6. Are task-oriented rather than self-oriented
7. Are open to newness and change
8. View and appreciate familiar things in new and different ways
9. Possess a sense of spirituality that connects them to all living things and the universe
10. Have empathy toward those from cultures other than their own
11. Relate to others as individuals
12. Have their own unique ethical sense of right and wrong
13. Resist acculturation
14. Are able to tolerate and enjoy silence and solitude
15. Are creative and inventive
16. Have a sense of humor and an appreciation of their own and other human failings

Maslow's theory of hierarchy of needs is demonstrated in pyramid format. Without the fulfillment of each level of these needs your mind will be too preoccupied to take action on the goals you have set out to accomplish and you will not develop to your highest potential. In other words, you will not have clarity in your thoughts to be creative to achieve your goals.

Dr. Maslow's theory of the hierarchy of needs is as follows:

Physiological Needs

At the base of the pyramid are our physiological needs of food, water, breathing, sleep, sex, warmth and excretion.

Once our physiological needs are met and are no longer controlling our behaviors, we move up to the second level of Maslow's pyramid.

Safety and Security

He describes these needs as being our need for security and stability of employment, safety of our body, and the security of organization and predictability. These are needs we fulfill when we are confronted with in a state of emergency.

The Need of Love and Belonging

These are the needs of giving and receiving love, friendship, family, and sexual intimacy. People seek to overcome feelings of loneliness. These needs must be satisfied before we can move up to the next level of esteem.

Esteem

This is the level of achievement, respect for ourselves and others, self-esteem and confidence. If these needs are not met then a feeling of inferiority and inadequacy will overwhelm our thoughts and we would be unable to move up to the next level of fulfilling the need of self-actualization.

Self-Actualization

When the four levels have been satisfied you have then reached the last level at the top of the pyramid. You are ready to fulfill the need to carry out your purpose and make the most of your life, or do what you were "born to do." Self-actualization is satisfying the need of life patterns, enrichment, adaptive flexibility, spontaneity, creativity, recreation and leisure.

Maslow's theory demonstrates that it is essential for humans to develop a foundation of fulfilled needs before the highest potential of success can be achieved.

Building your foundation contributes to your personal growth and his pyramid of self development points us in the direction of where to begin.

At the end of each day make a list in your journal of your daily accomplishments toward your personal foundation and growth towards self-actualization. Develop your own pyramid of satisfied needs and motivate yourself towards the accomplishment of your goal and prepare yourself to do what you were "born to do."

Epilogue

When you return to the previous pages of your journal entries, you will be astounded at the changes that have occurred in your life, the goals you have achieved, and the happiness you have brought to yourself and to others along the way. But most of all you will be amazed at growth and development towards your highest potential.

We all need hope and it is something that only we can create for ourselves. We are the only ones who can bring this wonderful concept into our lives. Creating hope begins with making small changes, and the small changes lead to bigger ones and a better life.

My quotes from Confucius indicate my respect for life as Confucius was a philosopher and an educator of humankind.

Confucius knew hundreds of years ago how we should be living our lives and many of us have yet to grasp the concept.

Respect your life as Confucius did and take action to make the necessary changes towards your eternal happiness.

"The superior man acts before he speaks, and afterwards speaks according to his action." Confucius **(551 BC-479 BC)**

Daily Journal

Date:

My daily shopping list of small goals:

My Goal:

My Vision of my goal:

Positive signs indicating the progress of my goal:

Road blocks I encountered indicating inconsistency in my thoughts and actions:

List of Fears:

Alternative thoughts to overcome my fears:

List of beliefs and knowledge about the goal:

List of what I did for myself to build my foundation:

Shopping List of positive things I did for others:

Your thoughts—empty your mind:

References

Richard Blonna, *Coping with stress in a changing world*, third edition, Copyright © 2005, 2000, 1996 by The McGraw-Hill Companies, Abraham Maslow, Hierarchy of Needs, p.27-28

Myers, G. David, *Exploring Psychology*, sixth edition, © 2005 by Worth Publishers, p.543, p343

Abraham Maslow, Hierarchy of Needs, p. 343 © 1999-2009

Philip G. Zimbardo, 1971 experiment www.zimbardo.com/zimbardo.html

A Course in Miracles © Copyright 1975, 1985, 1992, 1996 by the Foundation for Inner Peace, A Course in Miracles., fear, thoughts and perception, ego, self-love and forgiveness, knowledge and certainty, p. 4-43